Contents

Welcome to the Olympics! 4

Cities..10

Olympia 12

Olympic events 14

Ceremonies and feasts 20

On your marks, get set, go! 22

The modern Olympics..26

The story of the marathon..28

Timeline 29

Glossary 30

Want to know more? 31

Index...32

Some words are printed in bold, **like this**. You can find out what they mean on page 30. You can also look in the box at the bottom of the page where they first appear.

Welcome to the Olympics!

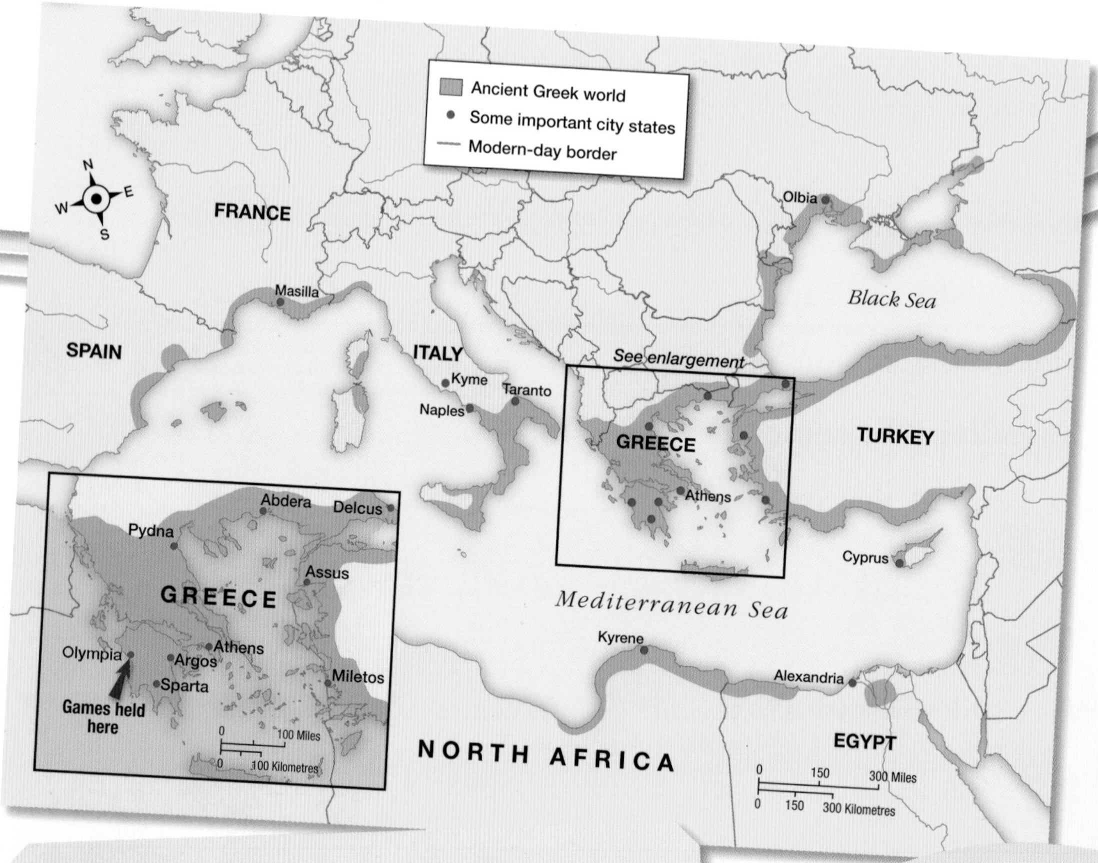
Ancient Greek world
Some important city states
Modern-day border
N
E
S
W
FRANCE
SPAIN
ITALY
Masilla
Kyme
Naples
Taranto
Olbia
Black Sea
See enlargement
GREECE
Athens
TURKEY
Cyprus
Mediterranean Sea
Kyrene
Alexandria
EGYPT
NORTH AFRICA
0 150 300 Miles
0 150 300 Kilometres
Abdera
Delcus
Pydna
Assus
GREECE
Olympia
Athens
Argos
Sparta
Miletos
Games held here
0 100 Miles
0 100 Kilometres

The time:
400 BC (about 2,400 years ago)

The place:
Olympia in ancient Greece

The sporting events:
Five days of races and competitions

The religious events:
Ceremonies (special actions) for the god Zeus

The competitors:
Top athletes from the Greek world

What to bring:
Gifts for Zeus

This is a map of the ancient Greek world. The countries on the map did not exist at the time of the ancient Greeks.

ceremony special actions, words, and music that people perform
festival special time of year when people meet together to have

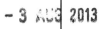

www.raintreepublishers.co.uk
Visit our website to find out more information about **Raintree** books.

To order:
☎ Phone 44 (0) 1865 888112
🖹 Send a fax to 44 (0) 1865 314091
💻 Visit the Raintree bookshop at **www.raintreepublishers.co.uk** to browse our catalogue and order online.

First published in Great Britain by Raintree,
Halley Court, Jordan Hill, Oxford OX2 8EJ,
part of Harcourt Education.

Raintree is a registered trademark of Harcourt Education Ltd.

Editorial: Louise Galpine and Claire Throp
Design: Richard Parker and Tinstar Design
    www.tinstar.co.uk
Illustrations: Steve Weston, Sebastian Quigley,
    International Mapping
Picture research: Mica Brancic
Production: Julie Carter

Originated by Modern Age
Printed and bound in China by Leo Paper Group

ISBN 978 1 4062 0764 4 (hardback)
12 11 10 09 08
10 9 8 7 6 5 4 3 2 1

ISBN 978 1 4062 0771 2 (paperback)
12 11 10 09 08
10 9 8 7 6 5 4 3 2 1

British Library Cataloguing in Publication Data
Bingham, Jane
Welcome to the Ancient Olympics!. – (Fusion)
796.4'8'0938
A full catalogue record for this book is available from the British Library

Acknowledgements

The publishers would like to thank the following for permission to reproduce photographs: AKG-images pp. **7** (Erich Lessing); Alamy/Visual Arts Library (London) p. **19**; Ancient Art & Architecture Collection Ltd pp. **9**, **13**, **23** (R Sheridan), **11**, **17** (C.M.Dixon); The Art Archive/Archaeological Museum Florence/Dagli Orti p. **14**; The Art Archive/National Archaeological Museum Athens/Dagli Orti p. **25**; The Art Archive/ Archaeological Museum Tarquinia/Dagli Orti p. **8**; The Bridgeman Art Library/British Museum, London, UK p. **24**; Corbis pp. **20** (Gianni Dagli Orti), **27** (Pete Saloutos).

Cover photograph of the Statue of Discobolus in front of the Athens Stadium, Greece, reproduced with permission of Alamy/Petr Svarc.

Every effort has been made to contact copyright holders of any material reproduced in this book. Any omissions will be rectified in subsequent printings if notice is given to the publishers.

The publishers would like to thank Nancy Harris and Michael Vickers for their assistance with the preparation of this book.

Disclaimer

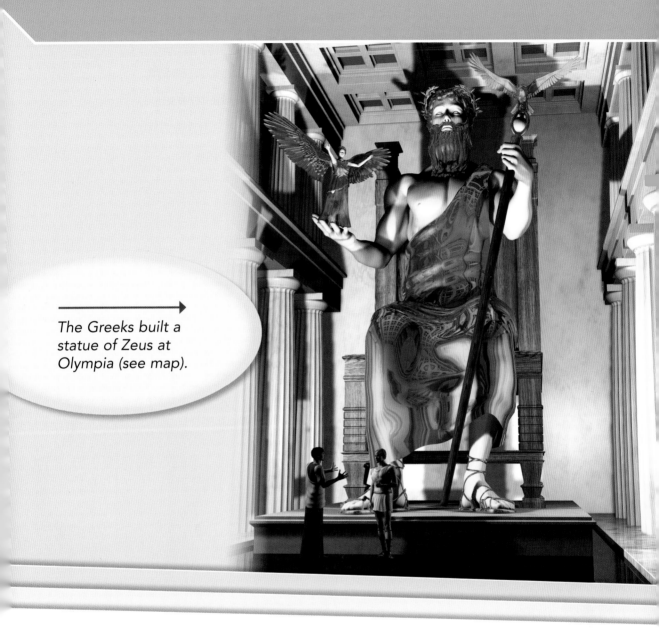

The Greeks built a statue of Zeus at Olympia (see map).

Who was Zeus?

The ancient Greeks had many gods. Zeus was their main god. The Greeks held a **festival** for Zeus at Olympia. This was an event that was held every year. This festival became the Olympic Games.

What's on at the Games?

At the ancient Olympics, there are some exciting **contests**. These might include a boxing match or a race. There are also some grand **ceremonies**. In one ceremony, competitors promise to compete with honour. They also promise to respect the rules.

Pentathlon and pankration

The **pentathlon** and the **pankration** are the toughest events. In the pentathlon, athletes compete in five different sports. In the pankration, contestants box and wrestle.

The Games at a glance

Day one: Opening ceremony and boys' events

Day two: Chariot races and pentathlon

Day three: Ceremony for Zeus and running races

Day four: Boxing, wrestling, and pankration

Day five: Prize-giving, feasts, and **celebrations**

chariot

celebration	special event to mark an important day
contest	another word for a competition
pankration	event where athletes fought against each other. It had almost no rules.
pentathlon	Olympic event with five different sports

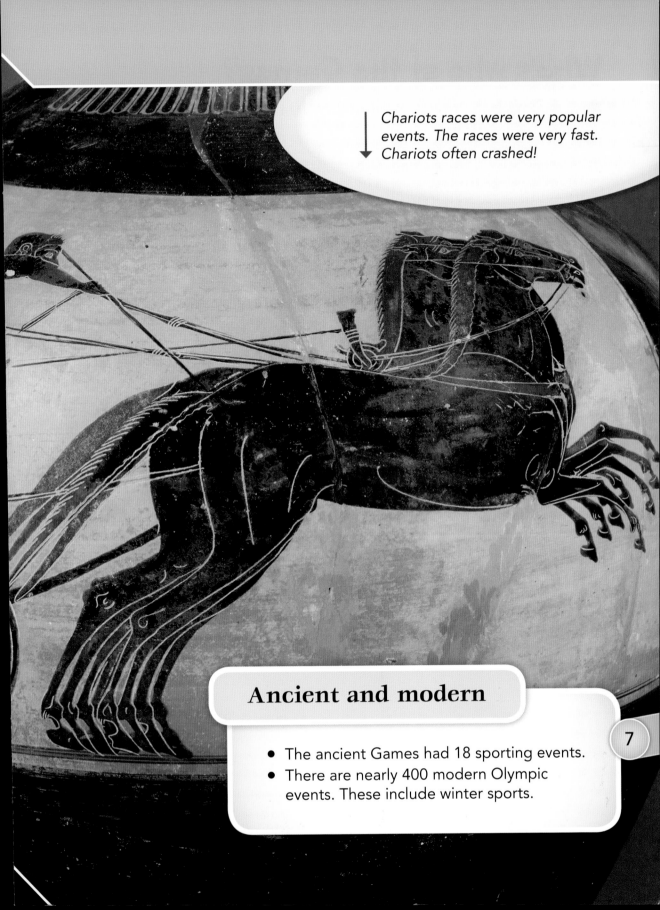

Chariots races were very popular events. The races were very fast. Chariots often crashed!

Ancient and modern

- The ancient Games had 18 sporting events.
- There are nearly 400 modern Olympic events. These include winter sports.

Who's who at the Games?

Athletes and trainers work out at Olympia. Athletes are very strong and fit. Trainers carry a long thin stick. They use their stick to point out what the athlete is doing wrong. Sometimes they give lazy athletes a smack!

Judges and priests (religious leaders) also spend time at Olympia. Judges have purple robes. Priests often wear white. All the judges come from Olympia. But they never favour the local athletes. Olympic judges are very fair.

This trainer is making sure the athlete is working hard.

Olympic contestants are usually men. But some strong girls run in special races.

Women at the Games

There are no grown-up women at Olympia. Only girls can watch the Games. A married woman cannot be in the crowd. If one is found she is thrown off a cliff!

There are a few running races for girls. These races are held in honour of Hera. She is the Greek goddess of girls and women.

Cities

People come from far away to compete. But everyone at the Games has one thing in common. All the athletes belong to a Greek **city state**. A city state is a large city and the farmland around it. Each one has its own ruler (leader).

Each city state has its own athletes. There is fierce competition between the states. Athens and Sparta are the biggest rivals.

A time of peace

A few city states are more than just sporting rivals. They also fight bloody wars against each other. But all the fighting stops during the Games. For a few weeks, there is a time of peace. This is known as the **Olympic truce**.

Olympic fact!

You wouldn't want to mess with an athlete from Sparta. Spartan babies are left out in the cold. This is to make them tough. Spartan boys and girls practise fighting every day.

city state large city and the farmland around it
Olympic truce time when all wars stopped in ancient Greece

Spartan warriors were famous for their strength.

Olympia

The stadium

The stadium is a huge rectangular area. It is surrounded by rows of seats. There are seats for about 45,000 people! Everyone in the stadium has a good view.

Some seats are made from earth. Some are made from stone. The seats made from earth are for anyone. The stone seats are kept for very important people!

This is a plan of how Olympia looked.

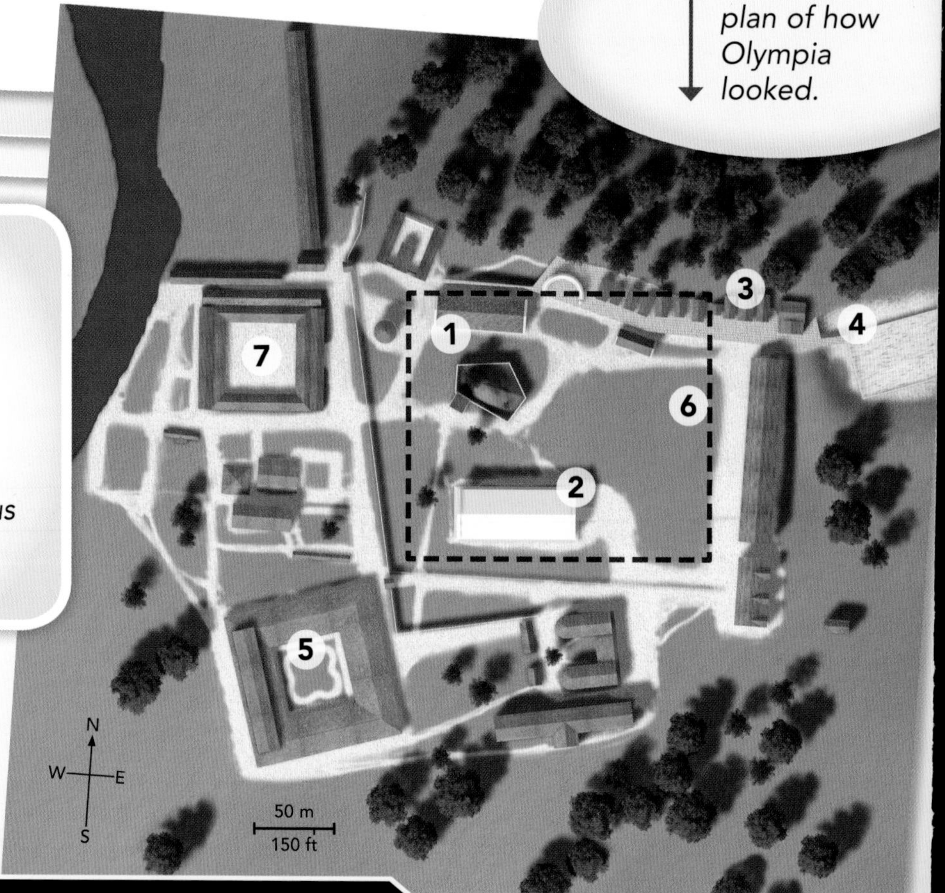

1 Temple of Hera
2 Temple of Zeus
3 The treasuries
4 The stadium
5 Athletes' centre
6 The sanctuary of Zeus
7 The Palaestra

50 m
150 ft

sacred holy, or to do with a religion
sanctuary very holy place

This was the Palaestra. The Palaestra was a training area for boxers and wrestlers.

The sanctuary

The **sanctuary** is a **sacred** (holy) space. The most important place is the Temple of Zeus. A temple is where people go to pray to the gods. The **treasuries** are places where gifts for Zeus are kept.

The Greeks believe that the Temple of Zeus marks a special spot. It is where Zeus threw a thunderbolt. He threw it because he was angry with the people on Earth!

Olympic events

Three running events are held on Day Three. One is the stadion. This is a quick sprint down one side of the stadium. This short race covers a distance of roughly 190 metres (208 yards). The longest race of the day covers 5,000 metres (3 miles). Athletes run 12 laps of the stadium.

This Greek dish shows an Olympic runner.

Test of strength

A real test of strength comes when all the runners have to wear armour. Runners wear a helmet and leg protectors. They also carry a heavy shield. A shield was used to protect a soldier's body in battle. Athletes run four laps of the stadium. Often they collapse before the end of the race.

Men who ran in armour were usually soldiers. The race was very good training for them.

Olympic fact!

Runners in armour carry a weight of up to 25 kilograms (55 pounds). That's like carrying more than 60 cans of baked beans!

Boxing and wrestling

On Day Four there is boxing and wrestling. The athletes often get some nasty **injuries**!

Greek boxing and wrestling are very dangerous sports. Boxers are allowed to hit an **opponent** when he is down. Wrestlers can break their opponent's fingers. Wrestlers are often covered with animal fat. The fat makes them greasy. This helps them to slip out of their opponent's grip.

The pankration

The violent **pankration** has almost no rules. Fighters are allowed to punch, bite, and scratch. They can even kick. The **contest** lasts until one fighter collapses or is killed.

Olympic fact!

In the pankration, fighters sometimes use their fingernails to rip out each other's eyes.

injury some kind of damage or harm to your body
opponent someone who is competing against you

Boxers wrap leather strips around their hands and wrists. This leaves their fingers free.

The pentathlon

The **pentathlon** is made up of five sports:

- throwing the discus
- hurling the javelin
- running
- long jump
- wrestling.

Only the best athletes take part in this event.

Athletes need great strength to throw the discus and the javelin. The discus is a flat, heavy disc. It is about the size of a dinner plate. It is usually made from stone, iron, or lead. The javelin is a metal-tipped wooden spear. It is as long as a man's body.

For the long jump, the athlete holds heavy stone weights. He holds a weight in each hand. First he jumps up. He holds out the weights in front of him. Then he comes down. He swings the weights behind him as he comes down. This helps to push him forwards.

Ancient and modern

- The ancient pentathlon sports are discus, javelin, running, long jump, and wrestling.
- The modern pentathlon sports are pistol shooting, fencing, swimming, horse riding, and cross-country running.

This athlete is about to throw a discus. He is taking part in the pentathlon.

Ceremonies and feasts

The Olympic Games are not just about sport. They are also an important religious event. The grand opening is very exciting.

Before the Games begin, there is a grand march. It goes to the Statue of Zeus. The athletes promise to obey the rules of the Games. They also swear that they have trained for at least 10 months.

Some athletes pray to Nike. She is the goddess of victory.

predict   tell the future
sacrifice   something that is killed and offered to
               the gods as a gift

Sacrifices often take place in the open air. Priests roast meat from an ox on the altar.

Honouring Zeus

On Day Three, everybody gathers at the Temple of Zeus.
The priest kills an ox. He looks at the animal's liver and heart.
They help him to **predict** (guess) who will win the Games.

Priests burn an ox on a large fire. The ox is a **sacrifice** to Zeus.
A sacrifice is a special gift to a god. The priests wait for the
smoke to rise to the heavens. Then they carve up the ox meat.
They serve it to the crowd.

On your marks, get set, go!

Olympic athletes have to train for at least 10 months. They also have to arrive 4 weeks early. This is for extra training at Olympia.

Olympic athletes spend many hours training. They work very hard. After they exercise, they are rubbed down with oil. Then they eat a huge meal!

Prizes and rewards

There are no money prizes at the ancient Olympics. Instead, the winner is given a simple crown. It was often made from olive leaves. Sometimes the **victor** is given ribbons. Winning athletes are treated like heroes in their home city. Sculptors make statues showing them in action. Poets write poems to praise their skill.

This athlete is a winner! He has been given ribbons as a prize.

victor   winner of a competition

Ancient and modern

- Nobody kept any records at the ancient Olympics.
- Record-keeping is a very important part of the modern Olympics.

Olympic superstars

Some amazing people competed in the ancient Greek Olympics. Here are just a few superstars.

Milo of Croton

Milo was a champion wrestler. He won the Olympic **victor's** crown six times. Milo trained by lifting a calf every day. The calf grew into a bull. Milo became very strong. Milo once saved his friends' lives. He held up the pillar of a falling building. His friends all escaped.

Wrestlers had to be extremely strong. ↓

↑ *Boxers usually hit out very hard.*

Melancomas of Caria

Melancomas was a famous boxer. He had an unusual style. He liked to dodge the blows of his **opponents**. He did this instead of hitting back. Melancomas could fight all day without a rest.

Aegeus of Argos

Aegeus won the long-distance race at Olympia. Then he ran straight home to tell the people of Argos. This journey involved running non-stop for around 96 kilometres (60 miles). Aegeus ran twice as far as a modern marathon runner!

The modern Olympics

The last ancient Olympics were held in AD 393. That was about 1,600 years ago. By this time, the Romans were running the Olympics. They liked more violent games. There was a gap of around 1,500 years. No Games were held.

In 1896, the first modern Games were held in Athens, Greece. This was the start of a new **series** (group) of Olympic Games.

The Olympic flame

Today, a team of **relay runners** carry a lighted torch from Olympia. They take it to the city where the Games are held. At the opening **ceremony**, the torch is used to light the Olympic flame. The flame burns all through the Games. The Olympic flame provides a link with the ancient (old) Olympics. During the ancient Games, a flame was kept burning in the Temple of Zeus.

It is a great honour to carry the Olympic torch.

The story of the marathon

The marathon is a running race in the modern Olympics. It covers about 42 kilometres (26 miles). The marathon was not part of the ancient Games. But it did begin in ancient Greece.

A marathon run

In 490 BC, the Greeks won a battle. It happened near the city of Marathon. The Greeks sent a messenger to Athens with the news. The messenger ran from Marathon to Athens. When he got to Athens, he said the word "Victory!". Then he collapsed and died.

Olympic marathons

The first marathon race was run in 1896. It was an event in the first modern Olympics. Runners raced from Marathon to Athens. They covered a distance of nearly 38 kilometres (24 miles).

In 1908, the Olympics were held in London. The runners in the London marathon ran an extra 3.2 kilometres (2 miles). After this race, the marathon covered about 42 kilometres (26 miles).

Timeline

BC

776

The first Olympic Games are held at Olympia. There is just one event – a short running race.

Around 720

A second running race is added to the Games. By this time the Games are held every four years.

632

The Olympics last for five days.

393

The Games are officially ended by the Roman Emperor Theodosius. This is the end of the ancient Olympics.

1924

The first Winter Olympics are held at Chamonix, France.

1960

The first Paralympics are held, for athletes with physical disabilities.

2008

The Olympics are held in Beijing, China.

2012

The Olympic Games will be held in London.

AD

1894

The International Olympic Committee (IOC) is founded.

1896

The first modern Olympics are held in Athens, Greece. Many new sports, including the marathon, are introduced.

1900

Women are allowed to take part in the Games.

Glossary

celebration special event to mark an important day. Birthday parties are celebrations.

ceremony special actions, words, and music that people perform. Some ceremonies are held in honour of a god.

city state large city and the farmland around it. In ancient Greece, there were several city states.

contest another word for a competition. You can take part in a swimming contest or a running contest for example.

festival special time of year when people meet together to have fun and remember an important event.

injury some kind of damage or harm to your body. Injuries can be minor, such as a sore finger, or very serious, like a broken neck.

Olympic truce time when all wars stopped in ancient Greece. During the truce everyone could enjoy the Olympic Games.

opponent someone who is competing against you. Opponents can be friendly or fierce.

pankration event where athletes fought against each other. It had almost no rules. In the modern Olympics, the pankration would be banned!

pentathlon Olympic event with five different sports. The pentathlon of the ancient Olympics is very different from the modern pentathlon event.

predict tell the future. A priest predicted who would win the Games.

relay runner member of a running team. Each relay runner runs for part of the way, before the next team member takes over.

sacred holy, or to do with a religion. Many religions have sacred places and sacred music.

sacrifice something that is killed and offered to the gods as a gift.

sanctuary very holy place. The word "sanctuary" can also mean a safe place, as in "animal sanctuary".

series group of related things that follow each other in order. The new series of Olympic Games began in 1896.

treasury place where treasure is kept. Another name for treasury is treasure house.

victor winner of a competition. Sometimes people use the word "victor" to mean the winner of a battle.

Want to know more?

Books to read

Ancient Greece and the Olympics, Mary Pope Osborne, Natalie Pope Boyce, Sal Murdocca (Random House, 2004)

Ancient Olympics, Jackie Gaff (Heinemann, 2003)

You Are There: You Are In Ancient Greece, Ivan Minnis (Raintree, 2005)

Websites

http://www.bbc.co.uk/schools/ancientgreece/
Two Greek children guide you around the ancient Olympics on this site.

http://www.perseus.tufts.edu/olympics/
This site includes sections on Olympia, famous athletes, and the different events at the Games.

www.historyforkids.org/learn/greeks/games/olympics.htm
This website takes a look at the ancient Olympic Games.

Read more about the ancient Romans in **Staying Alive in Ancient Rome**.

Read more about the people of ancient Egypt in **Reach for the Stars**.

Index

Aegeus of Argos 25
armour 15
Athens 10
athletes 8–9, 20, 22, 24–25

boxing 6, 13, 16, 17, 25

ceremonies 4, 6, 20–21, 26
chariot races 6, 7
city states 10

discus 18, 19

festivals 4, 5

gods and goddesses 4, 5, 9, 13, 20

Hera 9, 12

injuries and death 16

javelin 18
judges 8

long jump 18

marathon 28
Melancomas of Caria 25
Milo of Croton 24
modern Olympics 7, 18, 23,
    26–27, 29

Nike 20

Olympia 4, 5, 12–13

Olympic flame 26, 27
Olympic truce 10

Palaestra 13
pankration 6, 16
Paralympics 29
pentathlon 6, 18–19
priests 8, 21
prizes 22

record-keeping 23
relay runners 26
religious events 4, 20–21
rewards 22
running events 9, 14–15, 18, 25,
    28, 29

sacrifices 20, 21
sanctuary 13
soldiers 11, 15
Sparta 10, 11
sporting events 4, 6–7, 14–19, 29
stadium 12

temples 12, 13, 21
trainers 8
training 13, 22
treasuries 12, 13

winter sports 7
women and girls 9, 29
wrestling 6, 13, 16, 18, 24

Zeus 4, 5, 6, 12, 13, 20, 21